We Learn All About
Machines

A Complete Resource
for Preschool, Kindergarten,
and First Grade Teachers

by Sharon MacDonald

Fearon Teacher Aids
Simon & Schuster Supplementary Education Group

Editor: Marilyn Trow
Copyeditor: Kristin Eclov
Illustration: Pauline Phung
Design: Diann Abbott

ISBN 0-8224-4590-5

Printed in the United States of America
1.9 8 7 6 5 4 3 2

Contents

To the Teacher

Dear Teacher:

In this book you will find everything you need to introduce machines into your classroom. It is a complete unit packed full of background information and learning activities that will help you teach children about machines.

The materials are presented in four sections—About Machines, The Lever, The Wheel, The Inclined Plane, and Tools and Machines. You can pick and choose which topics you want to use. Each section contains an *introduction* and *activities*. The introductions give the basics of the topics, so there is little need for you to gather additional information on machines. The activities suggest projects for art time, snack time, play time, and learning time that correspond to and reinforce the topics. Since there are a number of activities listed for each topic, you can choose the ones that are appropriate for your class's skill level.

The *suggested reading* at the end of the teacher's guide lists reading and picture books that will enhance the children's enjoyment of machines. I suggest that when you introduce a topic, you also read one or two of the books to the children. You could also leave out picture books for the children to look at on their own.

The nine reproducible *worksheets* incorporate thinking and concept skills such as visual-discrimination skills and the fine-motor skills of drawing, cutting, and pasting. Suggestions for using the worksheets and the six reproducible *pattern pages* are included with the activities.

Have fun bringing machines to your classroom!

Sincerely,

Sharon MacDonald

TEACHER'S GUIDE

About Machines

INTRODUCTION

Any object that helps make work easier is a machine. Machines help people in two ways—they help us do work faster and they increase the amount of work that may be done. Machines are an important part of our lives. The earliest machines used were very simple tools, such as knives and axes. These tools increased the work people could do with their hands. Today, we still use simple machines. We also use complicated machines with many moveable parts—cars and other forms of transportation, televisions, telephones, lawn mowers, vacuum cleaners, and so on. These complex machines, however, are made of one or more of the following simple machines: the lever, the wheel and axle, the pulley, the ramp or inclined plane, the wedge, or the screw.

All machines need energy to work. Some machines, such as bicycles and scooters, are powered by the energy of humans. More complicated machines use different energy sources. Cars, trucks, and buses use gasoline. Windmills rely on the wind to provide the power to pump water from deep inside the ground. Trains and paddle-wheel boats are run by steam engines. The steam engines work when water is heated to the point of producing steam. Televisions and refrigerators need electricity to work. Scientists are experimenting with solar and nuclear energy as new, efficient sources of energy. Efficient energy will make it possible for us to accomplish more work in less time.

Today we live in a computerized age. Computers are machines that help us do tasks that we only dreamed of doing a few years ago. Computers are found in most businesses. Robots and other complicated machines used in manufacturing are computer-controlled. Airplanes and space shuttles are controlled by computers. Video games and other toys are computerized as well. Without machines, our lives would be very different.

ACTIVITIES

✿ Make a machines bulletin board. Display pictures of many different kinds of machines. Explain that machines are any items that help us do work. Help the children name each machine on display. Discuss how each machine makes work easier. Invite the children to illustrate their own ideas about how the machines may be used. Place a large 10" x 12" envelope near the bottom of the bulletin board for the children's drawings. Each day, randomly select one or more of the drawings from the envelope. Invite the children whose drawings were selected to share a story about their pictures with the rest of the class.

About Machines

ACTIVITIES

✿ Have a variety of simple machines available for children to investigate—a paintbrush (lever), a ramp (inclined plane), a doorstop (wedge), a screw, a pulley, and a wheel. Remind the children that all machines do special jobs. Point out that many machines have only a few parts. Explain that these machines have no motor and are operated by hand. Encourage the children to discuss each machine and the job it might be used for. Invite the children to think of new ways to use these machines.

✿ Remind children that all machines need energy to work. Invite the children to pretend to be wind-up machines. Collect several old keys. Group the children in pairs. Give a key to each pair. Have the partners take turns "winding" one another up and showing their versions of a machine. After a minute, suggest that the machines wind down. Invite several groups to perform for the entire class. Encourage the other children to guess the machines being acted out. When finished, place the keys in the music center. Play a tape of a variety of music. Invite the children to act as machines in time to the music.

✿ Invite the children to make machine collages. Collect assorted fasteners, pieces of electrical cord, and small machine parts from old toasters, blenders, vacuum cleaners, and similar appliances. Provide a styrofoam meat tray for each child (ask parents to wash and recycle). Invite each child to select several machine parts. Help the children arrange and glue the parts to the bottom of their trays. Then spray paint the parts and trays black. Display the collages on a classroom wall.

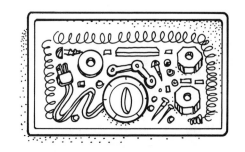

About Machines

ACTIVITIES

✿ Duplicate and hand out Worksheet 1 (page 27). Have the children color the picture according to the color key provided on the worksheet. When the children finish, discuss each colored shape. Place a picture of each shape on a bulletin board and write the name of the shape below each picture.

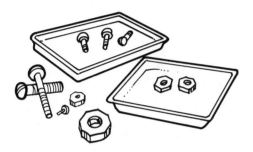

✿ Make a sorting game. Collect a variety of different sizes of nuts and bolts. Glue one of each size of nut and bolt on a styrofoam tray. Place the rest of the assorted nuts and bolts in a bowl. Encourage the children to sort the nuts and bolts by matching them to the nuts and bolts on the tray. Invite the children to sort the nuts and bolts using other attributes as well.

✿ Ask the children to name the machines they have in their homes (television, hair dryer, clock, bicycle, computer, and so on). Write each machine named on a strip of tagboard. Draw a simple picture as well. Encourage the children to explain how each machine helps them. Then hold up each tagboard strip, read the name of the machine printed on the strip, and ask the children to predict how their lives would be different if the machine no longer existed.

✿ Show the children a tape recorder. Ask the children to explain how a tape recorder makes work easier (it is faster than writing, allows people to listen to a recording while doing other tasks, and so on). Invite the children to take turns recording their ideas and thoughts about machines. When each child has had a turn, place the tape in the listening center.

About Machines

ACTIVITIES

✿ Bring in machines that are powered in different ways—a wagon or tricycle (human power), a kite (wind power), a record player (electricity), and, if possible, a lawn mower (gasoline engine). Show each machine to the children. Ask them to suggest ways to make the machines work. Encourage the children to name other machines powered by each of these energy sources. Then duplicate and hand out Worksheet 2 (page 28).

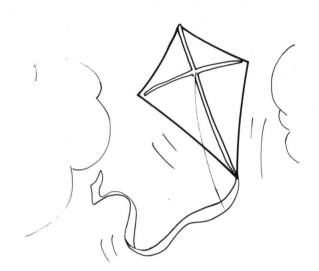

✿ Duplicate and hand out Worksheet 3 (page 29). Have the children identify and color the machines that are the same in each row.

✿ Show the children pictures of machines that make our lives easier. Encourage children to think of ways each machine helps us. Then ask the children how we might accomplish those tasks without the machines. Encourage the children to think about which machines, if any, they think they could do without. Then ask children which machines they feel are most important.

✿ Place two old telephones, a typewriter with paper, and a computer, if available, in a play center. Explain that the telephone, typewriter, and computer are machines. Encourage the children to discuss how these machines make work easier. Invite the children to practice calling one another on the telephone, typing letters, and using the computer for skill practice.

The Lever

INTRODUCTION

A lever is a bar that can be straight or bent. It is one of the oldest and simplest machines. Levers help people lift heavy objects. Pushing down on one end of a lever makes the other end go up in the air. A seesaw is a lever. Children sitting on opposite ends of the seesaw can lift each other's weight quite easily. It would be far more difficult for one child to lift another directly off the ground.

Levers are used in many ways. A screwdriver, when used to pry open cans or boxes, acts as a lever. Handles of paintbrushes, brooms, shovels, and other simple machines are levers as well. A tire jack works as a lever to raise a heavy car. Two levers combined make a double lever. Scissors, nutcrackers, pliers, and wrenches are double levers.

ACTIVITIES

✿ Point out that levers can be used to help people do all kinds of work. Explain that a bottle opener is a lever. Show the children a can of cocoa. Encourage the children to try opening the can with their fingers. After each child has tried, try opening the can with the bottle opener. Show the children how the bottle opener works like a lever to pry off the lid. Then make hot chocolate for a snack.

✿ If the playground at your school has a seesaw, take the children outside to experiment with this lever. Encourage the children to discuss how the seesaw makes the job of lifting another person much easier. Invite the children to experiment sitting at various places closer and farther away from the center of the seesaw. Challenge them to try lifting you as well!

The Lever

ACTIVITIES

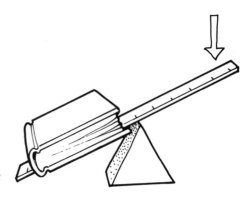

✿ Get a triangular block of wood (sides of equal length) approximately two inches wide, a wooden ruler, and a book. Challenge the children to try lifting the book using the materials provided. Guide the children to see that by balancing the wooden ruler on the top of the triangular block and placing the book on one end of the ruler, they can easily push down on the other end of the ruler and lift the book. Encourage the children to experiment with longer levers. Children should discover that longer levers can lift more weight.

✿ Fill a cardboard box with wooden blocks. Tape the box shut. Encourage the children to try lifting the box with their hands. Then using a broom handle as a lever, show the children how to lift the box.

✿ Hammer nails into a 2" x 12" x 24" board (approximately $1/2$" deep). Invite the children to try removing the nails with their fingers. Then show the children how to remove the nails using a claw hammer. Explain that the claw of the hammer acts as a lever.

✿ Explain to the children that the handle of a paintbrush is a lever. Give several children a large paintbrush (3" to 4" wide). Have several buckets of water handy as well. Invite the children to take turns painting a wall or sidewalk with water. Point out that the handle of the brush works as a lever. If possible, remove the handle of one of the brushes and invite the children to paint without the handle. Remind the children that since the brush makes work easier, it is considered a machine.

ACTIVITIES

✿ Use the patterns provided on page 39 to create a paint-brush seriation. Duplicate the patterns, color them, and then glue them on tagboard. Laminate the patterns for durability. Then cut out each brush. Help the children order the brushes from smallest to largest.

The Wheel

INTRODUCTION

The wheel and axle working together is one of the most important inventions of all time. The first wheels were probably rolling logs. Wheels make it easier and faster for us to move objects. They are also used in many kinds of complicated machines. Without wheels, our lives would not be the same. Wheels are used in bicycles, wagons, cars, trucks, buses, and other vehicles. They are also used in toys. Ferris wheels at carnivals are actually giant wheels. Wheels with teeth, called gears, are used to turn other wheels. This type of wheel is used in clocks, bicycles, and other similar machines.

A pulley is a wheel with a rope wrapped around it. Pulleys help lift objects and move them from place to place. One end of a rope is wrapped around the wheel and the other end is attached to an object. Flagpoles have pulleys to help people raise the flags. When a person pulls down on the rope, the flag goes up in the air. Pulleys also help us move heavy objects. Farmers use pulleys to raise bales of hay into the

hayloft. Pulleys are used in ski lifts to help skiers get to the tops of mountains. A drawbridge has a pulley that enables operators to raise and lower the bridge to allow boats to pass beneath it.

A machine that uses a pulley is called a crane. Cranes are often used to load cargo ships and to lift heavy building materials to the tops of tall buildings during construction projects.

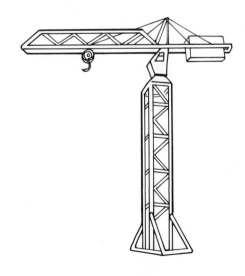

The Wheel

ACTIVITIES

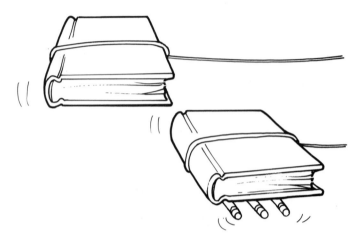

✿ Tie a piece of heavy string around a hardcover book approximately 8" x 10" x 1" high. Have the children take turns grasping the string and pulling the book across the table. Then place three pencils under the book and have the children try again. Discuss the difference the pencils make in moving the book.

✿ Cut out several six-inch circles from poster board. Cut a hole in the center of each (large enough for a pencil to fit through). If possible, take the children outside to the parking lot and show them a car. Point out the wheels and axles. Ask the children to explain why cars have wheels. When you return to the classroom, give each child two circles and a pencil. Show the children how to slide a circle over each end of the pencil. Then invite the children to roll their wheels and axles across the floor or table.

✿ Remind children that wheels are used in many ways. Help the children brainstorm a list of machines with wheels. Write each machine named on a strip of tagboard. Then help the children sort the tagboard strips according to the number of wheels each machine has. Duplicate and hand out Worksheet 4 (page 30).

✿ Get a cardboard box, a small wagon, and some bricks. Have the children load the bricks into the box and then push the box across the classroom. Have children unload the bricks from the box and load them into the wagon. Invite the children to pull the wagon back to the opposite side. Discuss which method is easier. Turn the wagon over and point out the wheels and axles.

The Wheel

ACTIVITIES

✿ Take the children on a "wheel watch walk." Take along a tape recorder. Encourage the children to look for wheels. Invite the children to dictate into the tape recorder as each wheel is spotted. When you return to the classroom, place the tape and recorder in the listening center for the children's enjoyment during independent time.

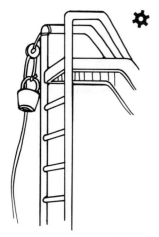

✿ Point out that a pulley is a wheel with a rope wrapped around it. Obtain a small, single-wheel pulley from a hardware store. Pass the pulley around the classroom and encourage the children to examine it. Take the children outside and attach the pulley to the top of the playground slide. Put a rope on the pulley and tie a bucket to one end of the rope. Place a large sheet of wax paper in the bucket. Have the children line up. Invite the first child to climb up the slide and sit at the top. Have the next child raise the bucket to the top of the slide by pulling on the free end of the rope and then lower the bucket when the child at the top removes the wax paper. Instruct the child at the top of the slide to take the sheet of wax paper from the bucket, sit on it, and slide down (the wax paper will make the child go down the slide faster). Have that child return the sheet of wax paper to the bucket and then raise and lower the bucket for the next child.

✿ Explain that wheels help objects move quickly and smoothly along a surface. Tie a length of clothesline rope above a door or chalkboard. Attach a single-wheel pulley to the rope. Then tie the other end of the rope to a chair so the rope slopes downward. A small basket may then be attached to the pulley. Invite the children to hold the basket on the high end of the rope and let go. Encourage the children to discuss what happens to the basket.

The Wheel

ACTIVITIES

✿ Take the children outside to the flagpole. Point out that the flag is raised and lowered by a pulley. Show the children how the pulley works on the flagpole. Invite each child to pull on the rope to move the flag a short distance. Encourage the children to imagine ways to raise the flag without a pulley.

The Inclined Plane

INTRODUCTION

Like the lever, the inclined plane (or ramp) makes moving heavy objects easier. An inclined plane is narrow on one end, then gradually slopes upward. Ramps are inclined planes that help people in wheelchairs gain easier access to buildings. Long ago, the Egyptians used inclined planes to move the heavy stones used to build the pyramids. Inclined planes are also used for play. A playground slide is an inclined plane. The staircase leading up to the slide is an inclined plane since the steps help people gradually climb. Different sizes and shapes of inclined planes are challenging and fun for people who enjoy riding skateboards. Inclined planes are useful in practical ways as well. Sloped roofs keep water and snow from accumulating on the tops of buildings.

The wedge is a type of inclined plane. Wedges force objects apart or hold them in place. A knife is a wedge. The sharp narrow side can slice through a substance. Pins and needles are also wedges. The sharp tips force the fibers of fabric or other material apart. Wedges are sometimes used to split firewood. A doorstop is another type of wedge. When the narrow end is forced under the door, the door is held open.

Another type of inclined plane is the screw. A screw is an inclined plane that goes around a center pole. Screws are very useful. They hold tighter than nails because the screw must be twisted before it can be removed. Screws can also raise objects. An old-fashioned piano bench moves up and down on a large screw located in its base. Cars can move down steep mountains at safe speeds when traveling on a road that spirals from the top to the bottom.

The Inclined Plane

ACTIVITIES

✿ Point out that the slide on the play-ground is an inclined plane. The slide helps the children reach the bottom slowly and safely. Invite the children to take turns on the slide. Explain that the steps leading up to the slide are an inclined plane because they make it easier to climb to the top.

✿ Bring a wagon and a few bricks to school. Put the bricks in the wagon. Take the children outside to a curb. Have the children take turns trying to pull the wagon over the curb. Then position a board from the street to the curb. Encourage the children to predict what will happen when they now try to pull the wagon over the curb. Invite children to check their predictions.

The Inclined Plane

ACTIVITIES

✿ Show the children pictures of people using ramps—moving vans, airplane conveyor belts, streets, driveways, skateboard ramps, and so on. Discuss how in each picture the ramp makes work easier. Encourage the children to look for examples of ramps in their communities and then share any discoveries with the rest of the class.

✿ Show the children a wedge (a triangular block). Explain that a wedge is a machine that makes it easier to spread items apart. Nail two blocks of wood together, leaving a narrow space between the blocks. Push the triangular block into the space between the blocks. Invite the children to take turns hammering the wedge until the two blocks of wood are driven apart.

The Inclined Plane

ACTIVITIES

✿ Invite the children to take turns using a dull table knife to cut small pieces of cheese for a snack. Show the children the blade of the knife. Point out that the blade is a wedge—it is tapered from the thin cutting edge to the wider top edge. Explain that the shape of the knife helps to push apart the cheese.

✿ Place a small hand saw and a large block of wood to be used in a block center with adult supervision. Saw a groove about $1/4$" deep in the block. Help each child use the saw to cut the wood block. Explain that the saw is a wedge because it causes the wood block to split apart.

✿ Fill a deep tray or tub with wet sand. Encourage the children to build a steep hill with the sand. Help them make a road that spirals from the bottom of the hill to the top. Point out that a spiral road makes it easier for cars to reach the top. It also makes it safe for cars to come down the hill. The turns slow cars down and make it easier for them to maintain safe speeds. Invite the children to drive toy cars and trucks along the new road.

✿ Show the children a large screw. Point out that screws, like other inclined planes, help us lift items. Hold the screw on a block of wood. Have a child hold one edge of a note card in the bottom groove of the screw (see right) as you slowly turn the screw to the right. Ask the children to observe closely and describe what happens. Then use a screwdriver to insert the screw in a soft block of wood. Point out the wood chips that the screw lifts up and out of the hole as it is screwed into the wood.

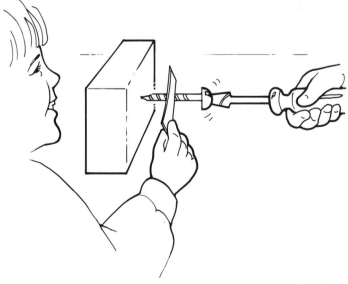

The Inclined Plane

ACTIVITIES

✿ Insert several screws of various sizes into a long board. Place the board and a screwdriver in the block center. Invite the children to use the screwdriver to screw the screws into the board and then back out again.

✿ Collect different sizes of bolts with fitting nuts. Separate the nuts and bolts. Then challenge the children to match the bolts and nuts by testing to see which nut fits each bolt.

Tools and Machines

INTRODUCTION

Some machines have many parts. Other machines, such as tools, have only a few parts. Tools are simple machines that need human energy to work. Tools save us time because they have been designed to do special jobs fast. Saws, hammers, shovels, and screwdrivers are a few of these special machines.

Many tools are made up of a combination of the six simple machines. Most tools, for example, have handles. The handles act as levers. A broom and dustpan are made up of a lever (broom handle), wedge (the dustpan separates the dirt from the floor), and inclined plane (the dustpan raises the dirt from floor level to the level of the dustpan). A knife is both a lever and a wedge. A pair of scissors is two levers put together with two sharp blades acting as

wedges. A rolling pin works much the same way as a wheel and axle.

We also have tools that help us build items. The claw on a hammer is a lever that may be used to pull nails out. The nail is really a simple machine. The sharp point of the nail is a wedge. It is small at the tip and gets bigger as it tapers upward along the shaft of the nail. Screwdrivers combine the lever (the handle) and wedge (the head). A hand drill is a combination of several simple machines—an inclined plane (the threads that twist around the shaft of the drill), a wedge (the drill tip), and a wheel and axle (the handle used to turn the drill). A saw is a wedge.

Many tools help people work in their yards and gardens. Hoes and shovels are combi-

Tools and Machines

nations of levers and wedges. The sharp ends of these tools are wedges and the handles are levers. Pruning shears used to trim trees and bushes are two levers working together.

Machines help people in many ways. People rely on machines for their transportation, play, communication, preparation of food, and other daily needs. Industries rely on robots and other complex machines to run factories efficiently. Machines will continue to play an important role in our lives. In the future, even more complex machines will be invented to make our lives easier and more energy efficient.

ACTIVITIES

✿ Duplicate and hand out Worksheet 5 (page 31). Review each simple machine and then instruct the children to draw a line from each simple machine to an example of how each machine might be used.

✿ Remind children that simple machines can be seen everywhere. Duplicate and hand out Worksheet 6 (page 32). Discuss the worksheet together in class. Help the children locate an example of a lever, pulley, inclined plane, and wheel and axle. Then invite the children to draw their own pictures showing the screw and wedge on the back of their worksheets.

✿ Take the children on a "machine walk" around the neighborhood. Encourage the children to listen for the sounds of machines. When you return to the classroom, discuss the various machine sounds heard. Listen for sounds of machines in the classroom and other places in school as well—pencil sharpener, typewriter, vacuum, computer, and so on. Help the children become aware of the machines around them.

✿ Explain that tools are special machines that are operated by hand. Help the children brainstorm a list of tools that might be used inside a home (fork, spoon, scissors), in a garden (hoe, shovel), and in a workshop (saw, hammer). Duplicate and hand out Worksheet 7 (page 33).

Tools and Machines

ACTIVITIES

❁ Duplicate and cut out the tool patterns provided on pages 40-41. Give each child one or more of the tool patterns. Have the children glue the tools on a sheet of construction paper.

❁ Play "Guess What?" Encourage each child to think of a tool that he or she could pantomime using. Call on various children to pantomime the actions of using the tools. Invite the other children to guess what tool each child pantomimes.

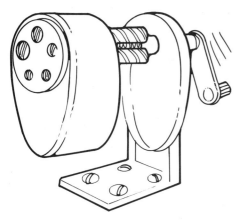

❁ Collect pictures of various machines. Show the pictures to the children. Encourage the children to discuss how the machines are alike and different.

❁ Point out that most machines are combinations of simple machines. Collect a variety of old magazines. Have children look through the magazines to find pictures of machines. Invite them to cut out the pictures. Back the pictures with tagboard and laminate them. Have children sort the pictures by the kind of work each machine does. Help the children identify the simple machines that make up the complicated machines.

❁ Help the children brainstorm a list of jobs. Encourage the children to discuss tools they think are necessary for each job they name. Remind children that most jobs require special tools. Ask them to share their ideas about the special tools used by members of their families in their jobs. Duplicate and hand out Worksheet 8 (page 34).

❁ Duplicate and hand out Worksheet 9 (page 35). Have the children select the most appropriate tool for each task.

Tools and Machines

ACTIVITIES

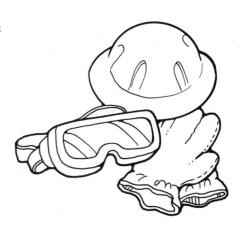

✿ Ask parents and other teachers if they might have an old toaster or other small appliance that they no longer want. Cut off the electrical cord. Remove any parts that may have sharp edges. Put the appliance and several tools in a learning center. Invite the children to use the tools to take the appliance apart. Invite children to use a variety of tools to "repair" broken toys or small electrical appliances from which the cords have been removed. Provide an apron, hard hat, safety goggles, and work gloves.

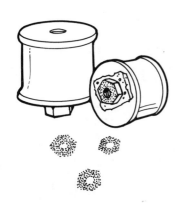

✿ Invite the children to invent their own machines. Duplicate and cut out the machine parts patterns provided on pages 42-43. Trace and cut out the parts on tagboard for durability. Make several copies of each part. Arrange the children into several small groups. Give each group sheets of construction paper, some paper fasteners, and copies of the machine parts. Encourage each child to arrange several of the machine parts on paper to make a machine. Help the children use paper fasteners to allow any wheels they might use to move. Glue several different sizes of nuts and bolts to small sponge squares. Glue a spool on the other sides of the sponges for handles. Suggest that interested children dip these sponges into tempera paint and print bolts and nuts on their machines. Ask the children to dictate the name and the purpose of their machines as well.

✿ Make robots. Duplicate and cut out several copies of the robot parts pattern provided on page 44. Trace the patterns on tagboard for durability. Place the parts on a table in a learning center. Invite the children to arrange several of the parts on sheets of paper to make robots. Remind the children that robots are machines and that machines make work easier. Encourage the children to share their robots with the class. Discuss how they help make work easier.

Tools and Machines

ACTIVITIES

✿ Read the following poem to the children. Then invite them to create imaginary machines. Collect many different sizes of boxes. Invite the children to glue the boxes together to make a machine. Provide pieces of cork, bottle caps, old knobs, colored wire, and other odds and ends that children might use to decorate their machines. Telephone companies will often donate leftover pieces of telephone cable to schools (split the cables open and inside you will find small colored wires). Help the children paint their finished creations. Encourage the children to name their machines and explain how the machines might make work easier.

Do Nothing Machine
By Sharon MacDonald

This story begins–
No blueprints or plans –
A rhyming account
Of a child's two hands.

It's the story about John,
The inventor of things,
Who made a machine
From wood, nails, and strings.

The nameless machine
Was built tall and wide.
The long nails stuck out
To tie string to each side.

With all kinds of tools,
John spent long hours
Reworking, remaking,
And adding tall towers.

When friends would ask John,
"What does it do?"
"Nothing," he'd say,
"I'm not even through."

John never quite finished
His lopsided do.
You just looked at it
As it stared back at you.

The *Do Nothing Machine*,
John named it one day
After months of adding. . .
and taking away!

The fun was in building,
Not getting through.
It was not important
what it could do.

Suggested Reading

Barton, Byron. *Building a House.* New York: Greenwillow Books, 1981. (K-2).

Burton, Virginia. *Mike Mulligan and His Steam Shovel.* Boston: Houghton Mifflin, 1987. (K).

Green, Carol. *Betsy and the Vacuum Cleaner.* New York: Random House, 1979. (K-1).

Hoban, Tana. *Push Pull Empty Full.* New York: Macmillan, 1972. (PS-K).

McLenighan, Valjean. *Stop-Go, Fast-Slow.* Chicago: Childrens Press, 1982. (PS-K).

Rockwell, Anne. "The House That Jack Built" from *The Three Bears and Fifteen Other Stories.* New York: Harper and Row, 1975. (K-1).

Rockwell, Anne and Harlow. *Machines.* New York: Macmillan, 1972. (PS-K).

Rockwell, Anne and Harlow. *The Toolbox.* New York: Macmillan, 1971. (K-1).

Wolde, Gunilla. *Tommy Builds a House.* Boston: Houghton Mifflin, 1971. (PS-K).

STUDENT
WORKSHEETS

Name _____

Find the hidden machines. Color the spaces.

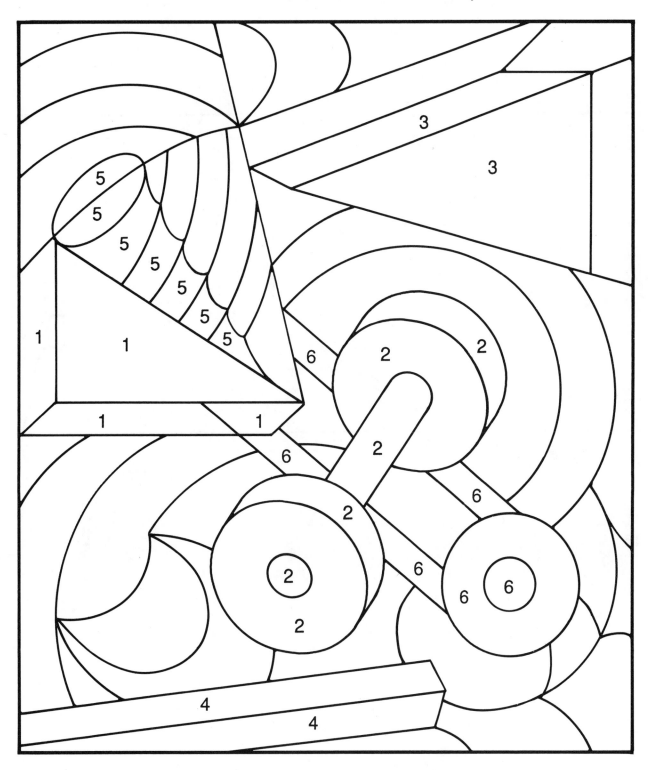

1 = red   4 = green
2 = yellow   5 = black
3 = blue   6 = brown

Skills: number and color recognition   27

Name _____

Connect the dots in order from 1 to 25.

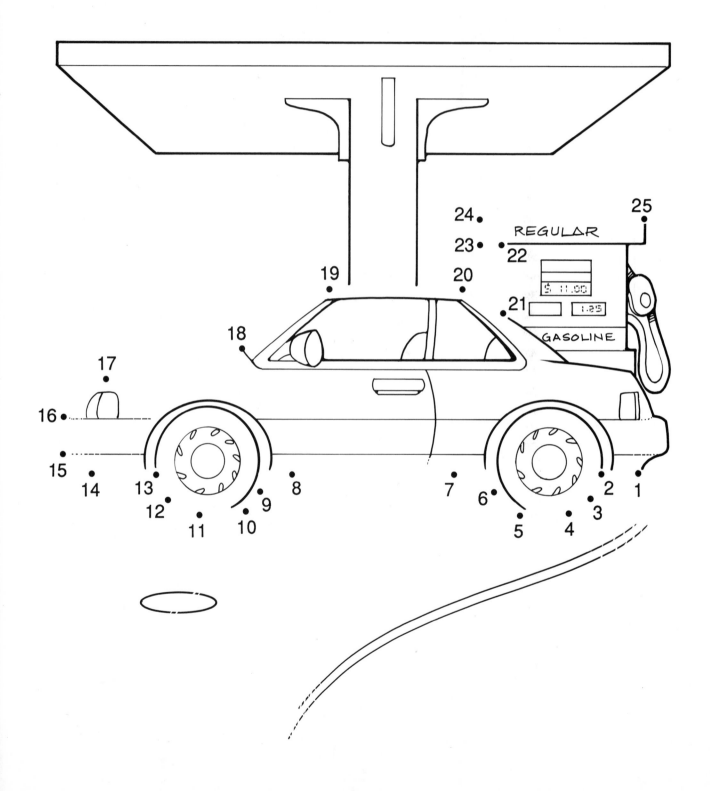

Skills: counting to 25, fine motor (drawing)

Name _____

Color the machines that are the same in each row.

Skills: understanding the concept of same, visual discrimination   29

Name _____

Color the wheels in the picture.

Skills: visual discrimination

Name _____

Match each simple machine with how it is used. Draw along each dotted line. Do not lift your pencil.

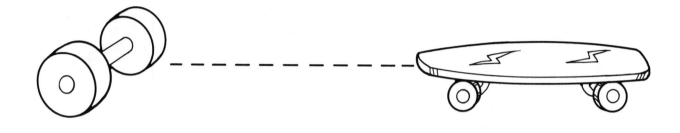

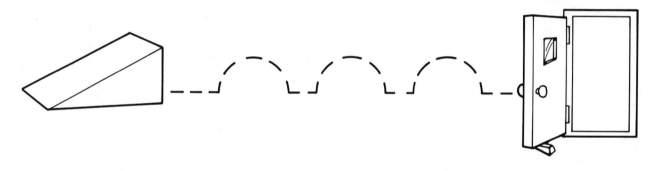

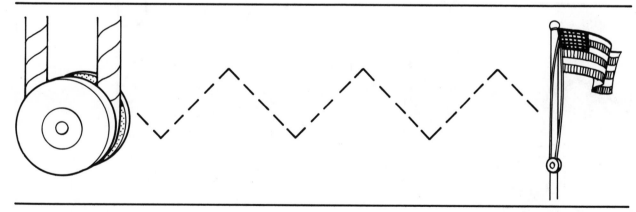

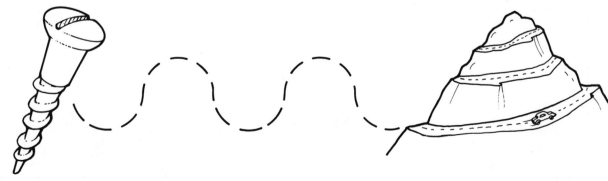

Name _____

Circle the simple machines.

Skills: visual discrimination, fine motor (drawing)

Name _____

Draw a line from the tools to the place where they would be used.

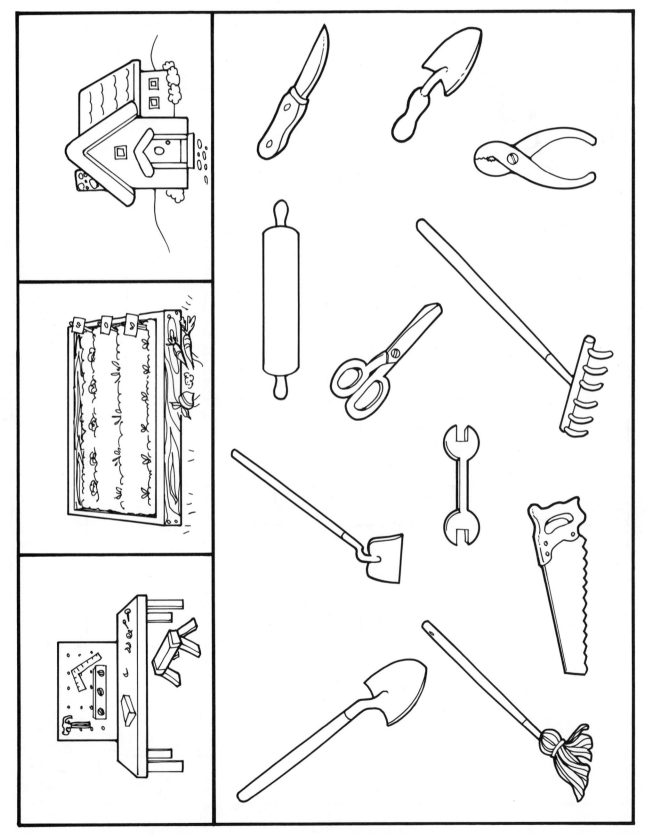

Skills: classifying, fine motor (drawing)

33

Name _____

Help the carpenter find his tools.

Skills: fine motor (drawing)

We Learn All About Machines © 1991 Fearon Teacher Aids

Name _____

Cut out the tool cards. Paste the tool cards
next to the job cards.

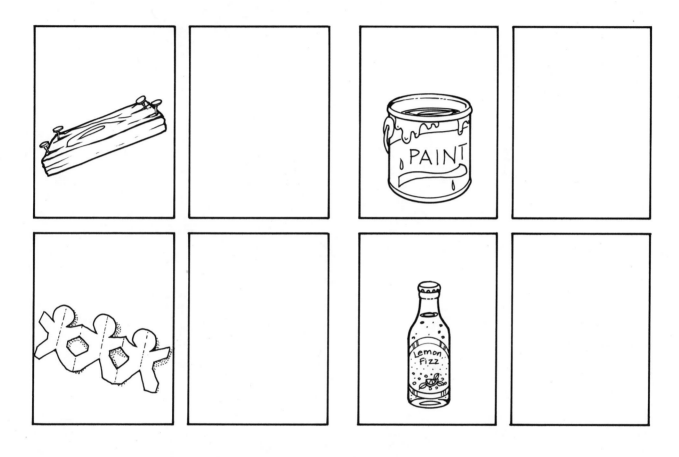

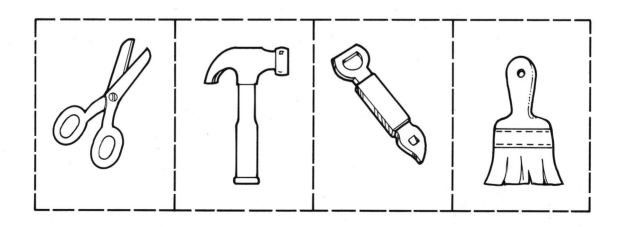

Skills: visual discrimination, fine motor (cutting and pasting)

PATTERN PAGES

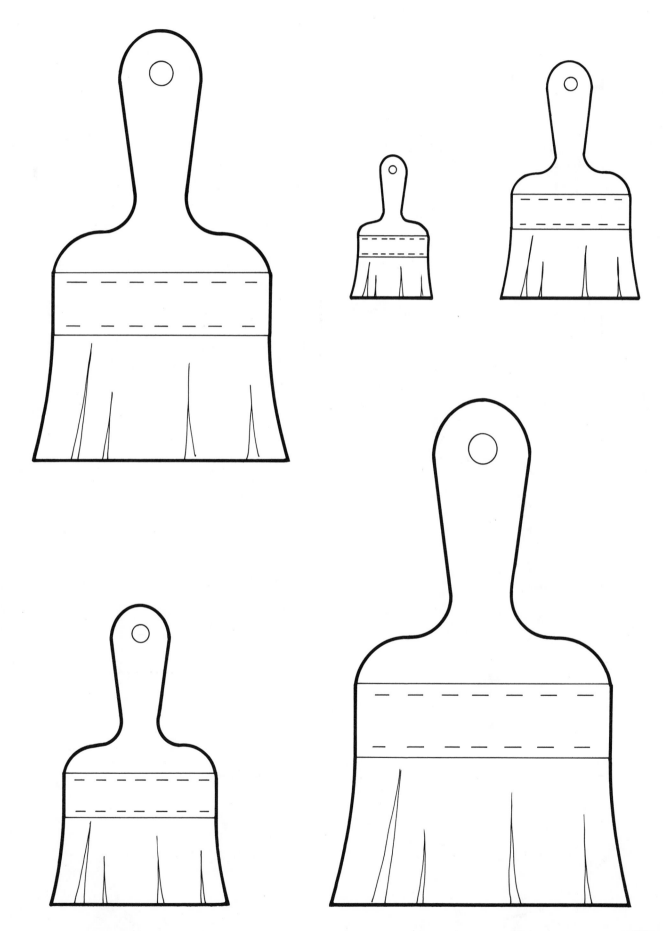

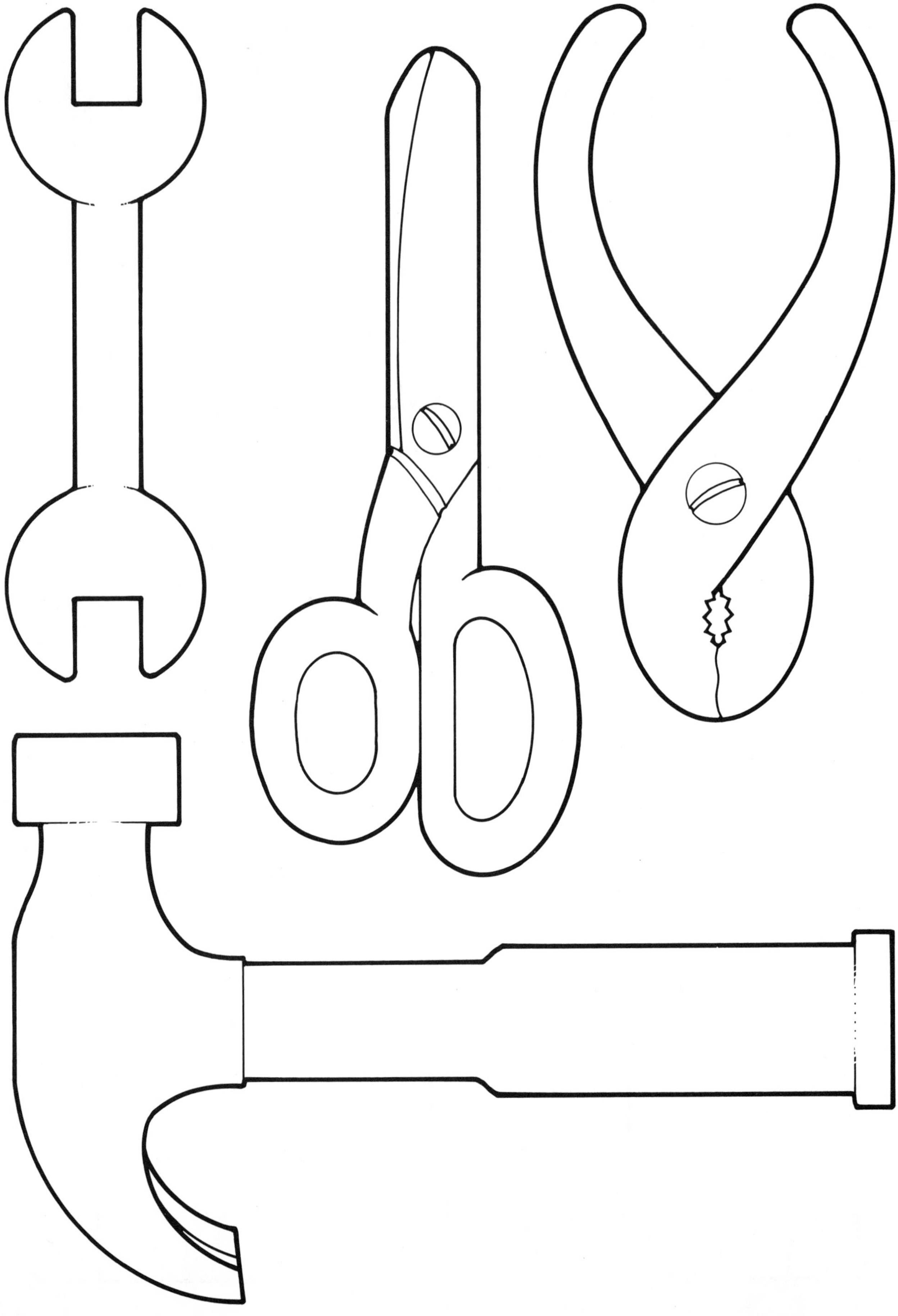

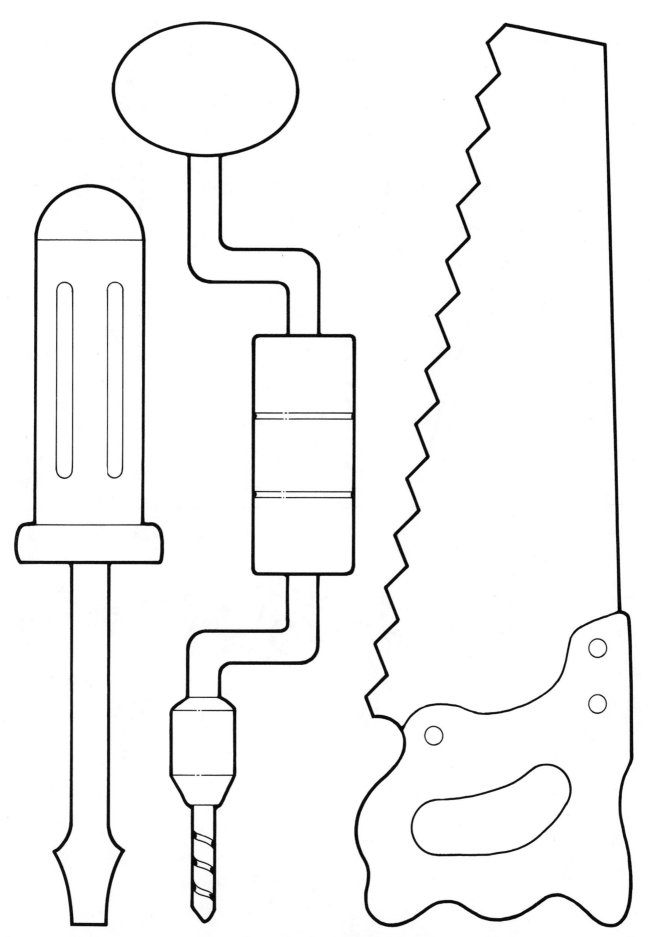

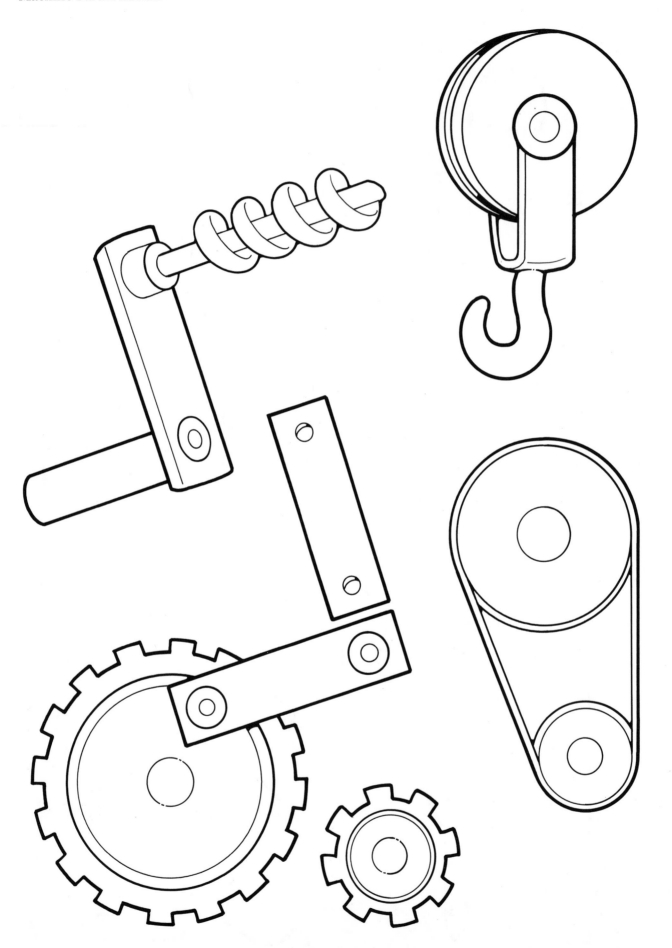

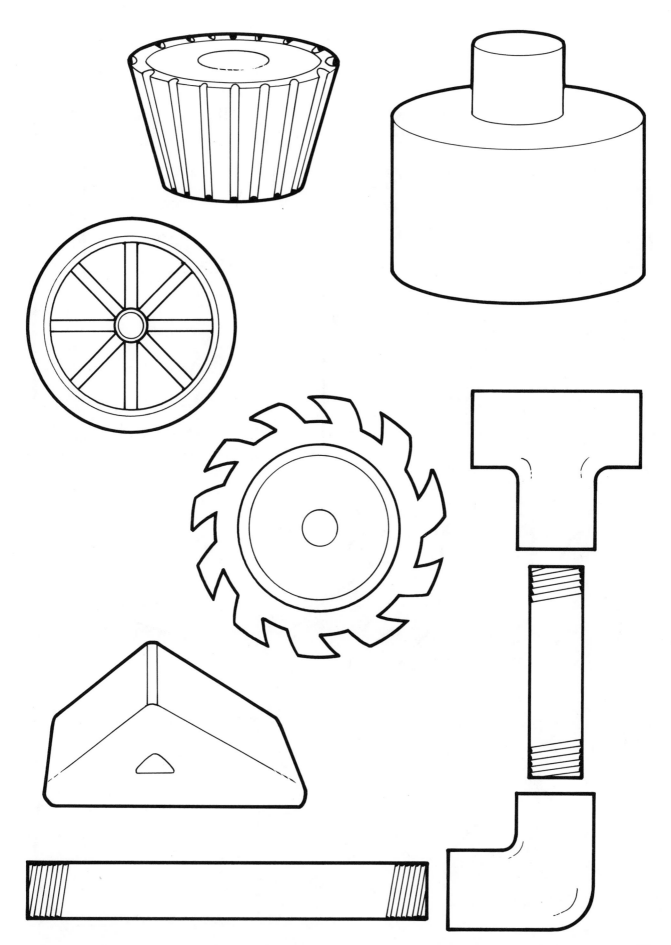

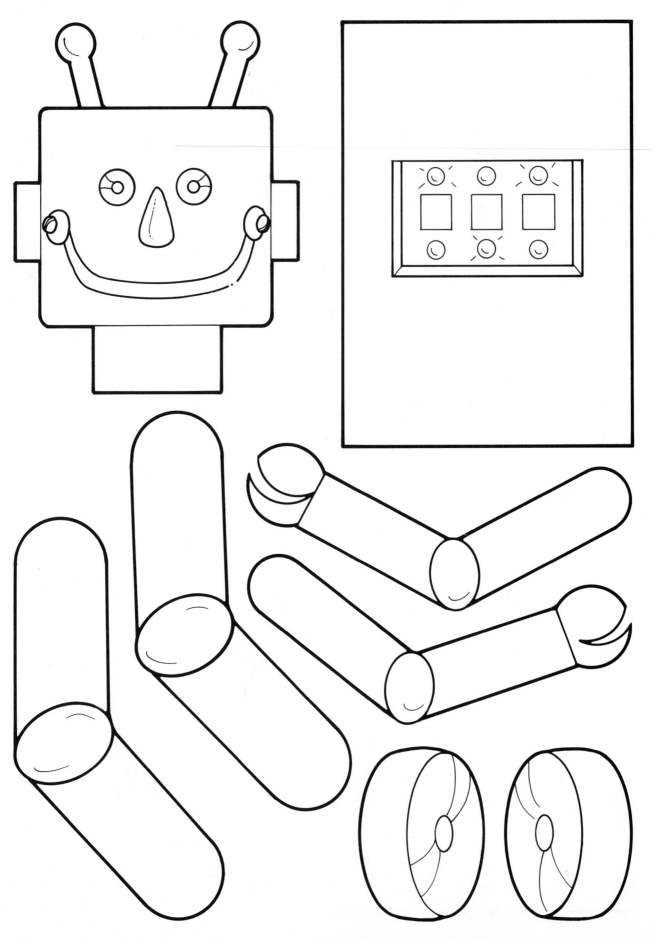